50 Tea Time in Japan Recipes

By: Kelly Johnson

Table of Contents

- Matcha Latte
- Sencha Green Tea
- Genmaicha (Brown Rice Green Tea)
- Hojicha (Roasted Green Tea)
- Japanese Black Tea (Wakocha)
- Sakuramochi (Cherry Blossom Rice Cake)
- Daifuku (Stuffed Rice Cake)
- Dorayaki (Red Bean Pancakes)
- Taiyaki (Fish-shaped Cake)
- Warabi Mochi (Bracken-starch Cake)
- Yatsuhashi (Cinnamon Rice Cake)
- Anpan (Sweet Bean Paste Bread)
- Castella Cake
- Matcha Madeleines
- Sweet Potato Cake
- Mizu Yokan (Jelly Dessert)
- Kuri Kinton (Sweet Chestnut Paste)
- Kashiwa Mochi (Oak Leaf Rice Cake)
- Jaga Batake (Potato Cakes)
- Kuzumochi (Kuzu Starch Cake)
- Goma Dofu (Sesame Tofu)
- Natsumikan Jelly
- Dorayaki with Matcha Filling
- Chiffon Cake (Matcha or Citrus)
- Mitarashi Dango (Sweet Soy Sauce Dumplings)
- Shingen Mochi (Water Cake)
- Kompeito (Sugar Candy)
- Kabocha (Pumpkin) Cheesecake
- Zunda Mochi (Edamame Paste Rice Cake)
- Yuzu Sorbet
- Black Sesame Soup
- Green Tea Ice Cream
- Soba Noodle Salad
- Sakura Jelly
- Sweet Bean Soup (Zenzai)

- Matcha Tiramisu
- Fruit Daifuku
- Kurikinton (Sweet Chestnut and Sweet Potato)
- Sencha Cookies
- Oshiruko (Sweet Red Bean Soup)
- Egg Custard (Chawanmushi)
- Grilled Rice Balls (Yaki Onigiri)
- Mochi Ice Cream
- Sweet Rice Pudding
- Chestnut Rice Cake
- Pancakes with Sweet Red Bean Paste
- Miso Caramel Bars
- Katsu Sandwiches
- Tamagoyaki (Japanese Omelette)
- Savory Japanese Pancakes (Okonomiyaki)

Matcha Latte

Ingredients:

- 1 teaspoon matcha powder
- 1 cup milk (dairy or non-dairy)
- 1 tablespoon honey or sweetener (optional)
- Hot water (about 2 ounces)

Instructions:

1. In a bowl, whisk matcha powder with hot water until smooth and frothy.
2. Heat the milk in a saucepan or microwave until hot, but not boiling.
3. Froth the milk using a frother or whisk.
4. Pour the frothed milk over the matcha mixture and stir gently.
5. Sweeten with honey or your preferred sweetener, if desired.

Sencha Green Tea

Ingredients:

- 1 teaspoon sencha green tea leaves
- 1 cup water (heated to about 160°F/70°C)

Instructions:

1. Place sencha green tea leaves in a teapot or infuser.
2. Heat water to approximately 160°F (70°C) and pour over the leaves.
3. Let steep for 1-2 minutes.
4. Strain and serve, enjoying the delicate flavors.

Genmaicha (Brown Rice Green Tea)

Ingredients:

- 1 teaspoon genmaicha tea (green tea with roasted brown rice)
- 1 cup water (heated to about 175°F/80°C)

Instructions:

1. Place genmaicha tea in a teapot or infuser.
2. Heat water to approximately 175°F (80°C) and pour over the tea.
3. Let steep for 2-3 minutes.
4. Strain and enjoy the nutty aroma and taste.

Hojicha (Roasted Green Tea)

Ingredients:

- 1 teaspoon hojicha tea leaves
- 1 cup water (boiling)

Instructions:

1. Place hojicha tea leaves in a teapot or infuser.
2. Bring water to a boil and pour over the leaves.
3. Let steep for 1-2 minutes.
4. Strain and serve hot, appreciating its unique roasted flavor.

Japanese Black Tea (Wakocha)

Ingredients:

- 1 teaspoon wakocha tea leaves
- 1 cup water (boiling)

Instructions:

1. Place wakocha tea leaves in a teapot or infuser.
2. Bring water to a boil and pour over the leaves.
3. Let steep for 3-5 minutes, depending on your desired strength.
4. Strain and enjoy its rich flavor.

Sakuramochi (Cherry Blossom Rice Cake)

Ingredients:

- 1 cup glutinous rice flour
- 1/2 cup water
- 1/4 cup red bean paste
- Salted cherry leaves for wrapping

Instructions:

1. Mix glutinous rice flour and water to form a smooth dough.
2. Divide the dough into small balls and flatten them.
3. Place a small amount of red bean paste in the center and fold the dough over to seal.
4. Wrap each ball with a salted cherry leaf.
5. Serve and enjoy the delicate flavor.

Daifuku (Stuffed Rice Cake)

Ingredients:

- 1 cup glutinous rice flour
- 1/2 cup water
- 1/4 cup sweet red bean paste (or any filling)
- Cornstarch for dusting

Instructions:

1. Mix glutinous rice flour and water to form a smooth dough.
2. Steam the mixture for about 20 minutes until cooked.
3. Dust your hands and working surface with cornstarch.
4. Divide the dough into small pieces, flatten them, and place a spoonful of filling in the center.
5. Fold the dough over the filling and seal it. Dust with more cornstarch to prevent sticking.

Dorayaki (Red Bean Pancakes)

Ingredients:

- 1 cup all-purpose flour
- 2 eggs
- 1/4 cup sugar
- 1/2 teaspoon baking powder
- 1/2 cup milk
- Sweet red bean paste for filling

Instructions:

1. In a bowl, whisk together flour, sugar, baking powder, and eggs until smooth.
2. Gradually mix in milk to form a batter.
3. Heat a non-stick skillet over medium heat and pour a small amount of batter to form pancakes.
4. Cook until bubbles form on the surface, then flip and cook until golden brown.
5. Spread red bean paste between two pancakes to create a sandwich.

Taiyaki (Fish-shaped Cake)

Ingredients:

- 1 cup all-purpose flour
- 1 tablespoon sugar
- 1/2 teaspoon baking powder
- 1 egg
- 3/4 cup milk
- Sweet red bean paste or custard for filling

Instructions:

1. In a bowl, mix flour, sugar, and baking powder.
2. Whisk in egg and milk until smooth.
3. Preheat a taiyaki pan and lightly grease it.
4. Pour batter into the fish-shaped molds, fill with red bean paste or custard, and cover with more batter.
5. Close the pan and cook over medium heat until golden brown on both sides.
6. Remove from the pan and serve warm.

Warabi Mochi (Bracken-Starch Cake)

Ingredients:

- 1 cup warabi starch (bracken starch)
- 1 cup water
- Potato starch or kinako (roasted soybean flour) for dusting
- Sugar (to taste)

Instructions:

1. In a pot, mix the warabi starch and water until smooth.
2. Heat the mixture over medium heat, stirring continuously until it thickens and becomes translucent.
3. Pour the thickened mixture into a flat dish and let it cool completely.
4. Once set, cut into bite-sized pieces and dust with potato starch or kinako to prevent sticking.

Yatsuhashi (Cinnamon Rice Cake)

Ingredients:

- 1 cup glutinous rice flour
- 1/2 cup sugar
- 1 teaspoon cinnamon
- 1/2 cup water
- Sweet red bean paste (for filling)

Instructions:

1. In a bowl, mix glutinous rice flour, sugar, and cinnamon.
2. Gradually add water, stirring until a smooth batter forms.
3. Steam the mixture for about 20 minutes until cooked through.
4. Once cooled, flatten the dough and place a small amount of red bean paste in the center.
5. Fold over and seal to form a dumpling shape.

Anpan (Sweet Bean Paste Bread)

Ingredients:

- 2 cups all-purpose flour
- 1/2 cup milk (warm)
- 1/4 cup sugar
- 1 teaspoon yeast
- 1/4 teaspoon salt
- 1 cup sweet red bean paste

Instructions:

1. In a bowl, combine warm milk, sugar, and yeast. Let it sit for 5-10 minutes until bubbly.
2. Add flour and salt, kneading until smooth. Let rise for about an hour until doubled in size.
3. Divide the dough into small balls, flatten them, and place a spoonful of red bean paste in the center.
4. Fold the dough over and seal, placing the seam side down.
5. Bake in a preheated oven at 350°F (175°C) for 15-20 minutes until golden brown.

Castella Cake

Ingredients:

- 1 cup all-purpose flour
- 1 cup sugar
- 1/2 cup milk
- 4 eggs
- 1/2 teaspoon honey
- 1 teaspoon baking powder

Instructions:

1. Preheat the oven to 350°F (175°C) and line a loaf pan with parchment paper.
2. In a bowl, whisk eggs and sugar until pale and frothy.
3. Mix in milk and honey, then gradually fold in flour and baking powder until just combined.
4. Pour the batter into the prepared pan and bake for about 30-35 minutes until a toothpick comes out clean.
5. Allow to cool before slicing.

Matcha Madeleines

Ingredients:

- 1/2 cup all-purpose flour
- 1/4 cup sugar
- 1/4 teaspoon baking powder
- 2 eggs
- 1/4 cup unsalted butter (melted)
- 1 tablespoon matcha powder

Instructions:

1. Preheat the oven to 350°F (175°C) and grease a madeleine pan.
2. In a bowl, whisk together flour, sugar, baking powder, and matcha powder.
3. In another bowl, whisk eggs until frothy, then mix in melted butter.
4. Combine the wet and dry ingredients until just mixed.
5. Fill the madeleine molds and bake for about 10-12 minutes until golden.

Sweet Potato Cake

Ingredients:

- 1 cup sweet potato (mashed)
- 1 cup all-purpose flour
- 1/2 cup sugar
- 1/4 cup butter (softened)
- 2 eggs
- 1 teaspoon baking powder
- 1/2 teaspoon vanilla extract

Instructions:

1. Preheat the oven to 350°F (175°C) and grease a cake pan.
2. In a bowl, cream together butter and sugar.
3. Add eggs and mix well, then stir in mashed sweet potato and vanilla extract.
4. Gradually add flour and baking powder until well combined.
5. Pour into the prepared pan and bake for 25-30 minutes until a toothpick comes out clean.

Mizu Yokan (Jelly Dessert)

Ingredients:

- 1 cup red bean paste
- 1/4 cup agar-agar powder
- 2 cups water
- Sugar (to taste)

Instructions:

1. In a pot, dissolve agar-agar in water over medium heat, stirring until it boils.
2. Add red bean paste and sugar, mixing until smooth.
3. Pour the mixture into a mold and let it cool to room temperature.
4. Refrigerate until set, then cut into squares for serving.

Kuri Kinton (Sweet Chestnut Paste)

Ingredients:

- 1 cup cooked chestnuts (peeled)
- 1/2 cup sugar
- 1/4 cup water

Instructions:

1. In a pot, combine cooked chestnuts, sugar, and water.
2. Cook over medium heat, mashing the chestnuts into a smooth paste.
3. Continue to cook until the mixture thickens to your desired consistency.
4. Let cool before using as a filling or side dish.

Kashiwa Mochi (Oak Leaf Rice Cake)

Ingredients:

- 1 cup glutinous rice flour
- 1/2 cup water
- Sweet red bean paste (for filling)
- Oak leaves (for wrapping)

Instructions:

1. In a bowl, mix glutinous rice flour and water until smooth.
2. Steam the mixture for about 20 minutes until cooked through.
3. Once cooled, divide the dough into small balls and flatten each piece.
4. Place a spoonful of sweet red bean paste in the center, fold, and seal.
5. Wrap each cake in an oak leaf and let them rest before serving.

Jaga Batake (Potato Cakes)

Ingredients:

- 2 cups mashed potatoes
- 1/2 cup all-purpose flour
- 1 egg
- Salt and pepper (to taste)
- Oil (for frying)

Instructions:

1. In a bowl, mix mashed potatoes, flour, egg, salt, and pepper until combined.
2. Shape the mixture into small patties.
3. Heat oil in a frying pan over medium heat.
4. Fry each patty until golden brown on both sides, about 3-4 minutes per side.
5. Drain on paper towels before serving.

Kuzumochi (Kuzu Starch Cake)

Ingredients:

- 1/2 cup kuzu (kuzu starch)
- 2 cups water
- Sweet syrup (for serving)

Instructions:

1. In a pot, mix kuzu with a little water to dissolve.
2. Gradually add the remaining water and heat over low heat, stirring continuously.
3. Cook until thickened and translucent, about 5 minutes.
4. Pour into a mold and let cool until set.
5. Cut into pieces and serve with sweet syrup.

Goma Dofu (Sesame Tofu)

Ingredients:

- 1 cup ground sesame seeds
- 1/2 cup water
- 1 tablespoon kuzu (kuzu starch)
- Salt (to taste)

Instructions:

1. In a bowl, mix ground sesame seeds, water, kuzu, and salt until smooth.
2. Pour the mixture into a pot and cook over low heat, stirring continuously until thickened.
3. Once thickened, pour into a mold and let cool.
4. Cut into cubes and serve with soy sauce or other dipping sauces.

Natsumikan Jelly

Ingredients:

- 2 cups natsumikan juice (or any citrus juice)
- 1/4 cup sugar
- 2 teaspoons agar-agar

Instructions:

1. In a saucepan, combine natsumikan juice, sugar, and agar-agar.
2. Heat the mixture over medium heat until it boils, stirring to dissolve the agar-agar.
3. Pour into a mold and let it cool to room temperature.
4. Refrigerate until set, then cut into squares for serving.

Dorayaki with Matcha Filling

Ingredients:

- 1 cup all-purpose flour
- 1/2 cup sugar
- 2 eggs
- 1 teaspoon baking powder
- 1/4 cup water
- Sweet matcha red bean paste (for filling)

Instructions:

1. In a bowl, whisk together flour, sugar, eggs, baking powder, and water until smooth.
2. Heat a non-stick pan over medium heat and pour small circles of batter.
3. Cook until bubbles form on the surface, then flip and cook until golden brown.
4. Place a spoonful of matcha red bean paste between two pancakes to form a sandwich.

Chiffon Cake (Matcha or Citrus)

Ingredients:

- 1 1/2 cups all-purpose flour
- 1 cup sugar
- 1/2 cup vegetable oil
- 6 eggs (separated)
- 1/2 cup water
- 1 tablespoon matcha powder or zest of citrus (for flavor)
- 2 teaspoons baking powder

Instructions:

1. Preheat the oven to 325°F (160°C) and prepare a chiffon cake pan.
2. In a bowl, mix flour, sugar, baking powder, and matcha (or citrus zest).
3. In another bowl, whisk egg yolks, oil, and water until smooth.
4. Combine the wet and dry ingredients, mixing until smooth.
5. In a separate bowl, beat egg whites until stiff peaks form, then gently fold into the batter.
6. Pour the batter into the prepared pan and bake for about 50-60 minutes until a toothpick comes out clean.

Mitarashi Dango (Sweet Soy Sauce Dumplings)

Ingredients:

- 1 cup glutinous rice flour
- 1/2 cup water
- 1/4 cup soy sauce
- 2 tablespoons sugar
- 1 teaspoon cornstarch (for glaze)

Instructions:

1. In a bowl, mix glutinous rice flour and water to form a dough.
2. Shape the dough into small balls and thread them onto skewers.
3. Boil the dumplings in water until they float, about 3-5 minutes.
4. In a saucepan, combine soy sauce, sugar, and cornstarch, heating until thickened.
5. Grill or pan-fry the dumplings briefly, then brush with the sweet soy sauce glaze before serving.

Shingen Mochi (Water Cake)

Ingredients:

- 1 cup kuzu (kuzu starch)
- 2 cups water
- 1/2 cup sweet syrup (such as brown sugar syrup)
- Kinako (roasted soybean flour)

Instructions:

1. In a pot, dissolve kuzu in 1 cup of water.
2. Gradually add the remaining water and heat over low heat, stirring constantly until it thickens.
3. Pour the mixture into a mold and let it cool until set.
4. Once cooled, cut into pieces and serve with sweet syrup and kinako.

Kompeito (Sugar Candy)

Ingredients:

- 2 cups granulated sugar
- 1/2 cup water
- Food coloring (optional)

Instructions:

1. In a pot, combine sugar and water and heat over medium heat, stirring until sugar dissolves.
2. Allow the mixture to simmer without stirring until it reaches a syrupy consistency.
3. Remove from heat and let cool slightly.
4. If desired, add food coloring and stir gently.
5. Pour the syrup onto a baking sheet and allow it to harden before breaking into pieces.

Kabocha (Pumpkin) Cheesecake

Ingredients:

- 1 1/2 cups cooked kabocha (pumpkin)
- 1 package (8 oz) cream cheese, softened
- 1/2 cup sugar
- 2 eggs
- 1 teaspoon vanilla extract
- 1/2 teaspoon cinnamon
- 1 pre-made graham cracker crust

Instructions:

1. Preheat the oven to 350°F (175°C).
2. In a bowl, mix kabocha, cream cheese, sugar, eggs, vanilla, and cinnamon until smooth.
3. Pour the filling into the graham cracker crust.
4. Bake for 30-35 minutes until set.
5. Let cool before slicing and serving.

Zunda Mochi (Edamame Paste Rice Cake)

Ingredients:

- 1 cup cooked glutinous rice
- 1 cup shelled edamame (cooked and cooled)
- 1/4 cup sugar
- A pinch of salt
- Cornstarch (for dusting)

Instructions:

1. In a food processor, blend cooked edamame, sugar, and salt until smooth.
2. Mix the glutinous rice with the edamame paste until well combined.
3. Dust your hands and a work surface with cornstarch.
4. Shape the mixture into small balls and dust with more cornstarch to prevent sticking.

Yuzu Sorbet

Ingredients:

- 1 cup yuzu juice
- 1/2 cup sugar
- 1 cup water
- A pinch of salt

Instructions:

1. In a saucepan, combine sugar, water, and salt, heating until the sugar dissolves completely.
2. Remove from heat and stir in yuzu juice.
3. Pour the mixture into a shallow dish and freeze for about 2 hours, stirring every 30 minutes.
4. Once fully frozen, scrape with a fork to create a fluffy texture before serving.

Black Sesame Soup

Ingredients:

- 1 cup black sesame seeds
- 4 cups water
- 1/2 cup sugar
- A pinch of salt

Instructions:

1. Toast black sesame seeds in a dry pan until fragrant, then grind them in a food processor until smooth.
2. In a pot, combine ground sesame, water, sugar, and salt.
3. Heat over medium heat, stirring constantly until thickened, about 10-15 minutes.
4. Serve warm in bowls.

Green Tea Ice Cream

Ingredients:

- 2 cups heavy cream
- 1 cup whole milk
- 3/4 cup sugar
- 4 egg yolks
- 2 tablespoons matcha powder

Instructions:

1. In a saucepan, heat cream, milk, and sugar until warm.
2. In a bowl, whisk egg yolks. Slowly add the warm milk mixture to the yolks while whisking.
3. Return the mixture to the saucepan and cook over low heat until thickened.
4. Stir in matcha powder until well combined.
5. Chill the mixture in the refrigerator, then churn in an ice cream maker until set.

Soba Noodle Salad

Ingredients:

- 8 oz soba noodles
- 1/4 cup soy sauce
- 2 tablespoons sesame oil
- 1 tablespoon rice vinegar
- 1 carrot (shredded)
- 1 cucumber (julienned)
- 2 green onions (chopped)
- Sesame seeds (for garnish)

Instructions:

1. Cook soba noodles according to package instructions; drain and rinse with cold water.
2. In a bowl, whisk together soy sauce, sesame oil, and rice vinegar.
3. Toss the cooled soba noodles with the dressing, carrot, cucumber, and green onions until well combined.
4. Garnish with sesame seeds before serving.

Sakura Jelly

Ingredients:

- 1 cup cherry blossoms (sakura), pickled or salted
- 2 cups water
- 1/2 cup sugar
- 1 tablespoon agar-agar powder

Instructions:

1. Rinse the cherry blossoms thoroughly to remove excess salt.
2. In a pot, combine water and sugar, and bring to a boil.
3. Stir in agar-agar until dissolved.
4. Add the rinsed cherry blossoms and let simmer for a few minutes.
5. Pour the mixture into molds and let cool until set in the refrigerator.

Sweet Bean Soup (Zenzai)

Ingredients:

- 1 cup adzuki beans
- 3 cups water
- 3/4 cup sugar
- A pinch of salt
- Mochi (for serving)

Instructions:

1. Rinse the adzuki beans and soak them in water overnight.
2. Drain and add the beans to a pot with 3 cups of fresh water.
3. Bring to a boil, then reduce to a simmer until the beans are tender (about 1-2 hours).
4. Stir in sugar and salt, and simmer for another 10 minutes.
5. Serve warm with mochi pieces.

Matcha Tiramisu

Ingredients:

- 1 cup heavy cream
- 1/2 cup mascarpone cheese
- 1/2 cup sugar
- 2 tablespoons matcha powder
- 1 cup brewed matcha tea (cooled)
- Ladyfinger biscuits

Instructions:

1. Whip heavy cream, mascarpone, and sugar until soft peaks form.
2. In a separate bowl, mix cooled matcha tea and matcha powder.
3. Dip ladyfinger biscuits in matcha tea and layer them in a dish.
4. Spread a layer of the cream mixture over the biscuits.
5. Repeat layers and refrigerate for at least 4 hours before serving.

Fruit Daifuku

Ingredients:

- 1 cup mochiko (sweet rice flour)
- 1/2 cup sugar
- 1 cup water
- Fresh fruits (such as strawberries, peaches, or kiwi)
- Cornstarch (for dusting)

Instructions:

1. In a bowl, mix mochiko, sugar, and water until smooth.
2. Steam the mixture for about 20 minutes until it becomes translucent.
3. Allow it to cool slightly and then knead until smooth.
4. Dust your hands and a surface with cornstarch.
5. Divide the dough into pieces, flatten them, and wrap around the fruit.

Kurikinton (Sweet Chestnut and Sweet Potato)

Ingredients:

- 1 cup sweet potatoes (peeled and cubed)
- 1/2 cup cooked chestnuts (peeled and chopped)
- 1/4 cup sugar
- A pinch of salt

Instructions:

1. Boil sweet potatoes until tender, then drain and mash them.
2. In a bowl, mix the mashed sweet potatoes with sugar, salt, and chestnuts until well combined.
3. Shape into small balls or patties and serve warm or at room temperature.

Sencha Cookies

Ingredients:

- 1 cup all-purpose flour
- 1/4 cup powdered sugar
- 1/4 cup butter (softened)
- 1 tablespoon sencha green tea leaves (finely ground)
- 1 egg yolk

Instructions:

1. Preheat the oven to 350°F (175°C).
2. In a bowl, cream together butter and powdered sugar until light and fluffy.
3. Add flour, sencha tea leaves, and egg yolk, mixing until a dough forms.
4. Roll the dough into small balls and flatten them on a baking sheet.
5. Bake for 10-12 minutes until lightly golden.

Oshiruko (Sweet Red Bean Soup)

Ingredients:

- 1 cup adzuki beans
- 3 cups water
- 1/2 cup sugar
- Mochi (for serving)

Instructions:

1. Rinse adzuki beans and soak overnight.
2. Drain and place beans in a pot with water, bringing to a boil.
3. Simmer until beans are soft (about 1-2 hours).
4. Stir in sugar and cook for another 10 minutes.
5. Serve warm with mochi.

Egg Custard (Chawanmushi)

Ingredients:

- 2 eggs
- 1 cup dashi (Japanese soup stock)
- 1 tablespoon soy sauce
- 1 teaspoon mirin
- Fillings (such as shrimp, chicken, and mushrooms)

Instructions:

1. In a bowl, beat the eggs gently and mix with dashi, soy sauce, and mirin.
2. Strain the mixture to remove air bubbles.
3. Place fillings in small cups and pour the egg mixture over them.
4. Steam the cups over simmering water for about 15-20 minutes until set.

Grilled Rice Balls (Yaki Onigiri)

Ingredients:

- 2 cups cooked rice (preferably short grain)
- Salt
- Soy sauce or miso (for brushing)

Instructions:

1. While the rice is still warm, shape it into triangular or round balls and season with a little salt.
2. Preheat a grill or pan over medium heat.
3. Grill the rice balls for about 2-3 minutes on each side, brushing with soy sauce or miso as they cook.
4. Serve warm as a snack or side dish.

Mochi Ice Cream

Ingredients:

- 1 cup mochiko (sweet rice flour)
- 1/4 cup sugar
- 1 cup water
- Ice cream (any flavor)
- Cornstarch (for dusting)

Instructions:

1. In a bowl, mix mochiko, sugar, and water until smooth.
2. Steam the mixture for about 20 minutes until it becomes translucent.
3. Allow it to cool slightly and then knead until smooth.
4. Dust your hands and a surface with cornstarch.
5. Divide the dough into small pieces and flatten each piece to wrap around a small scoop of ice cream.
6. Freeze until set.

Sweet Rice Pudding

Ingredients:

- 1 cup sweet rice (mochi rice)
- 4 cups water
- 1/2 cup sugar
- 1/2 teaspoon salt
- Cinnamon or vanilla extract (optional)

Instructions:

1. Rinse sweet rice under cold water until the water runs clear.
2. In a pot, combine sweet rice and water.
3. Bring to a boil, then reduce heat and simmer until the rice is tender and creamy (about 30-40 minutes).
4. Stir in sugar, salt, and cinnamon or vanilla if desired.
5. Serve warm or chilled.

Chestnut Rice Cake

Ingredients:

- 1 cup sweet rice flour
- 1/2 cup sugar
- 1/2 cup water
- 1 cup chestnuts (cooked and chopped)
- Cornstarch (for dusting)

Instructions:

1. In a bowl, mix sweet rice flour, sugar, and water until smooth.
2. Fold in the chopped chestnuts.
3. Pour the mixture into a greased dish and steam for about 30 minutes until set.
4. Allow to cool and cut into squares, dusting with cornstarch to prevent sticking.

Pancakes with Sweet Red Bean Paste

Ingredients:

- 1 cup all-purpose flour
- 1 tablespoon sugar
- 1 teaspoon baking powder
- 1 cup milk
- 1 egg
- Sweet red bean paste (for filling)

Instructions:

1. In a bowl, mix flour, sugar, and baking powder.
2. In another bowl, whisk together milk and egg.
3. Combine wet and dry ingredients until just mixed.
4. Heat a skillet over medium heat and pour in batter, cooking until bubbles form.
5. Spoon sweet red bean paste onto one half of the pancake and fold over.
6. Cook for an additional minute, then serve warm.

Miso Caramel Bars

Ingredients:

- 1 cup butter (softened)
- 1 cup brown sugar
- 1 cup granulated sugar
- 1 cup all-purpose flour
- 1/2 cup miso paste
- 1 teaspoon vanilla extract

Instructions:

1. Preheat the oven to 350°F (175°C) and grease a baking dish.
2. In a bowl, cream together butter, brown sugar, granulated sugar, and miso paste until smooth.
3. Mix in flour and vanilla until combined.
4. Pour the batter into the prepared dish and smooth the top.
5. Bake for 25-30 minutes until golden and set.
6. Allow to cool, then cut into bars.

Katsu Sandwiches

Ingredients:

- 2 pork cutlets (or chicken)
- 1 cup panko breadcrumbs
- 1/2 cup flour
- 1 egg (beaten)
- Bread (for sandwiches)
- Tonkatsu sauce (for serving)

Instructions:

1. Dredge each cutlet in flour, dip in beaten egg, and coat with panko breadcrumbs.
2. Heat oil in a skillet over medium heat and fry the cutlets until golden and cooked through (about 4-5 minutes per side).
3. Drain on paper towels and slice the cutlets.
4. Assemble sandwiches with bread, sliced katsu, and drizzle with tonkatsu sauce.

Tamagoyaki (Japanese Omelette)

Ingredients:

- 4 eggs
- 2 tablespoons sugar
- 1 tablespoon soy sauce
- 1 teaspoon mirin
- Oil (for frying)

Instructions:

1. In a bowl, whisk together eggs, sugar, soy sauce, and mirin until well combined.
2. Heat a non-stick skillet and lightly oil it.
3. Pour a thin layer of the egg mixture into the skillet and cook until just set.
4. Roll the omelette toward one side of the skillet, then add another layer of egg mixture to the empty side.
5. Continue rolling and adding layers until all the egg mixture is used.
6. Allow to cool slightly, then slice into pieces.

Savory Japanese Pancakes (Okonomiyaki)

Ingredients:

- 2 cups all-purpose flour
- 1 cup dashi (or water)
- 1 cup cabbage (shredded)
- 1/2 cup green onions (chopped)
- 1/2 cup meat (pork or shrimp, optional)
- Okonomiyaki sauce (for serving)
- Mayonnaise (for serving)

Instructions:

1. In a bowl, mix flour and dashi until smooth.
2. Stir in cabbage, green onions, and meat if using.
3. Heat a skillet and pour in the batter, shaping it into a pancake.
4. Cook until the bottom is golden, then flip and cook until the other side is golden.
5. Serve topped with okonomiyaki sauce and mayonnaise.

www.ingramcontent.com/pod-product-compliance
Lightning Source LLC
LaVergne TN
LVHW081505060526
838201LV00056BA/2943